Mastering Japanese Form Poetry and the American Haiku

Mastering Japanese Form Poetry and the American Haiku

For Lovers Who Write

E. Owen

4-Point Omega Publishing

Brooklyn, New York

Universal Poet E. Owen, currently living in Brooklyn, New York, is the author and publisher of this book of poems.

Copyright © 2022 by 4-Point Omega Publications. All rights reserved.

No portion of this publication may be reproduced or transmitted in any form or by any means, electronically, mechanically, by photocopying, computed copying to the cloud or uploading to retrieval systems or websites or IaaS, by downloading by any party or pasting or recording or otherwise without prior written expressed permission from its author and publisher.

Poetry - Intended for older adolescents and adults.

ISBN: 979-8-9854010-0-4

Editing, layout, text, and cover design by 4-Point Omega Publications.

Cover editing and formatting by Amazon KDP and 4-Point Omega Publications.

Cover Illustration: Traditional Oriental Ink Painting, sumi-e

(black-ink painting), Adobe Illustration licensed 2022,

Adobe Stock #281793876

E-book manufacturing by Amazon KDP.

To my beloved, whomever you are and were, whenever you were, and wherever you are or will be found.

Acknowledgements

Encyclopedia Britannica and its editors and contributors have provided the most easy-to-comprehend authority for this subject matter. In their words: they "oversee subject areas in which they have extensive knowledge whether from years of experience gained by working on that subject content or via study for an advanced degree . . ." While they have not contributed to this work individually, I trust their collective commitments and academia for personal guidance and clarification regarding this subject matter.

Contents

Table of Content

Acknowledgement	vi
Preface	xv-xvii

Introduction	1
Poetry for Lovers Who Write	15
Complicated	15
Love Letter	16
Paradox	16
Love Letter	17
Yearning	17
It's Only Fair	18
Longing for You	18
With You	19
Without You	19
Kiss Me	20
Seemly Hearts	20

Juliet Teases	21

E. Owen

Romeo's Persistent	21
Romeo Continues	21
Juliet	22
Romeo Hesitates	22
Juliet Replies	22
Romeo's Heart	22
Juliet's Heart	23
Romeo's Oath	23
Juliet's Answer	23
Romeo's Fate	23
Juliet	24
Romeo's Good Night	24
Juliet Pauses	24
Romeo Vows	24
Juliet Next Morning	25
Romeo	25
Juliet	25
Romeo Ascends	25
Juliet	26

Contents

Romeo Past Noon	26
Juliet	26
Juliet Next Day	26
Romeo	27
Juliet	27
Romeo's Troth	27
Juliet	27
Romeo Next Day	28
Juliet's Nurse	28
Romeo's Sorrow	28
Juliet's Nurse	28
Romeo's Farewell to Juliet	29
Juliet's Nurse	29
Romeo	29
Juliet's Nurse	29
Romeo Confused	30
Juliet's Nurse	30
Juliet Appears	30
Romeo's Pride	30

E. Owen

Juliet's Sorrow	31
Romeo Replies	31
Juliet's Joy	31
Missed Heaven	32
Don't Go	32
Sacred Heart	33
Connecting	34
Allow Me	34
Our Talks	35
Sun-lit Moon	35
Call	35
Love You	36
Not Like That	36
Candid Poses	37
Chagrin	38
Peccant Lines	38
Peace Bond Rose	39
Yellow Petal	39
M	40

Contents

Loves Floods	40
A Love for Spring	41
Softly	41
Accidental Love	41
Yes	42
Nocturnal Flower	42
Mm Yes	42
Trust	43
Resignation	43
Love Letter	43
Love Chooses	44
Secrets	44
Oh Gahd Daamn!	45
Love Letter	45
Uncertainty	46
Love in Winter	46
Comfort Me	46
Willing	47
Imperfect	47

E. Owen

Loveless	47
Lie With Me	48
Come Over	48
Imbue Me	48
If Love Declared	49
Whisper	49
Tuesdays	49
Cheated Hearts	50
No Pride	50
Making Plans	51
Distant Lover	51
Envy	52
Guilty Pleasure	52-53
Ginkgo Love	53
The Way We Do	53-54
Fun	54
Unloved	55
Lotus Lover	55-56
Her	56-57

Contents

Saturated Love	57-58
Yin and Yang	58-59
Waxing Poetic	59-60
Candid Stare	60
No Place to Go	61
Lovers Till Dawn	62
Love Letter	62
Metaphor For Love	63
For Lovers Only	64
I Do	64
Plump for Love	65
Father Time	65
Still My Heart	66
Unloved Heart	67
Never Have, Never Will	68
Your Love and I	69
From Me to You	70
Lily Daffodil	71
Reborn	72

E. Owen

Give Me Courage	72
Lover's Twilight	73
Noble Heart	74
Sources	75-77
Appendix	78
SHST	78
NOTES	

Preface

Preface

Some years ago, when I first began writing the haiku form, I delved into the whole issue about correct structure and components for the elusive, traditional, Japanese haiku. Interest in various forms of haiku was growing rapidly on social media, and poets from around the world were chiming in at on-line haiku challenges and sharing ideas with the rest of the world. So, why was writing 3 lines and 17 syllables causing such a stir for haiku enthusiasts in the western world, and how many forms of haiku were keeping with Japanese tradition? Was keeping with tradition really the focus of so much indulgence? Well, after witnessing traditional, Japanese haiku of 3 lines with less than 17 syllables, what exactly did traditional haiku look like? Confusion, to say the least. So, I soon realized that the enormous amount of information, as well as misinformation about this specific triplet—although often well intentioned—was, at the very least, too much to digest and extremely time consuming for fast-paced Westerners who just wanted to get in on the fun of on-line challenges and enjoyment of writing haiku. Nevertheless, my alpha-sigma senses were as relentless as the myriad English interpretations teaching the process for writing haiku. Amid the myriad interpretations came Japanese syllabaries, treatises on Japanese language and its Chinese origins, and the Japanese phonetic system with its English equivalent—if one even existed. It all read like an "Undergrad'" syllabus of history, fact, fiction, and phonetics, and all I wanted to do was justice to writing haiku. So, I gathered my wits and turned to

E. Owen

Oxford and other English references for a simpler, more consistent, and authoritative interpretation to crown my previous, well-spent endeavors. Eventually, I found my landing pad at Encyclopedia Britannica, whose great work I have decided to share with you in this book, as I guide you on a journey to writing your best haiku and other types of Japanese form poetry tailored to perfection for poets in the western world. For me, haiku and other types of Japanese form poetry are meditative. Syllabic formatting in Japanese form poetry requires we consider our choice of words before writing. It often inspires us to seek alternatives and build vocabulary, consider current and new perspectives of where we are in a moment, and where we are day to day in our personal lives and experiences. Creating within a form requires a collaboration between limitation and freedom of expression, wherein we yield to form, and, at the same time, enjoy freedom to recreate the form within the form itself. You might conceptualize this collaboration as a "yin and yang" relationship, like yielding and, at the same, excelling like coexisting opposites sharing one space, and like finding patience in frustration. Japanese form poetry is like therapy by the numbers. I write form poetry for the peace of mind and Zen-like focus and clarity I can achieve, both on the journey of writing a piece, and at the end of a completed work, whether the work is one poem or a book of poems like this one. I have been inspired in a positive way by Japanese form poetry, and hope that with my help you will be inspired as well.

Mastering Japanese Form Poetry and the American Haiku

Introduction

Poetry is

imaginable, like a spirit in a séance, an epiphany from an incantation, a plop from a pebble entering a pond, and the end of the ripple the pebble creates. First it stirs, then it speaks to enlighten, creates a ripple in time, then is once again still.

Poetry can be all those occurrences in a single moment captured in a world of words carefully selected, which, by their poet's nature, become poetry from the poet's penned comprehension of life's implicit sphere of communication, often divulging the unspoken word of the poetic soul.

It is therefore an epistemological doctrine of communication, whereby inferiority and superiority collaborate in defiance of limitation and authority, to balance life in a universal instance we call "poetry."

Japanese Form Poetry

Hello, fellow poets and interested readers! Thank you for purchasing *Mastering Japanese Form Poetry and the American Haiku: For Lovers Who Write,* and welcome to a comprehensive view into the world of Japanese form poetry from a Westerner's point of view. For many aspiring poets, various forms and structures required for writing Japanese form poetry are difficult to master, especially if they are further complicated by deciphering Japanese syllabaries and phonetics, translating Japanese terminology to English equivalents, pronouncing Japanese names, and remembering historic origins of Japanese poetry. Also, while I have your attention on form, I feel necessity to inform you that poetry can take many forms not readily obvious to readers who read without technical poetics guiding them. For example, this introduction will cover external sentence, line, and syllabic structural forms, but internal forms such as metaphorical, fictional, and metaphysical can also guide a reader poetically. Nevertheless, getting back to the broader topic, having spent countless hours figuring how Japanese syllabaries and phonetics play a role in writing Japanese form poetry, I have concluded that as I share a love for linguistics with many in the field and enjoy the task of learning how language other than my own language works, I am at last a Westerner in every aspect of my life, including poetry. With that epiphany, I have come to realize that American poets prefer their poetic efforts are not confined to a box: for example, controlled by metrical structures for validity. America's contemporary poet tends to prefer more freedom to explore multi-rhythmic structures in a single line, opposing, for example, one rhythmic structure per line or poem. One example of said box is the iambic metrical structure some say is required for writing traditional, Japanese haiku. The contemporary focus, however, when creating Japanese form poetry, tends to be more on perfecting syllabic structure, rather than perfecting limitations within metrical structures and traditional Japanese themes. Contemporary poets prefer that rhythmic structures come from the poet's pulse and relationship with words and affect at the time their words are chosen with specificity. The pulse creates a relationship between the words and the poet. Therefore, if a

Mastering Japanese Form Poetry and the American Haiku

poet's pulse creates a relationship with a string of words, which consequently give rise to a rhythmic line consisting of spondaic (stressed/stressed), Iambic (unstressed/stressed), and trochaic (stressed/unstressed), rhythmic structures, the poet's pulse polysemy (i.e., string of words with more than one rhythmic pulse) is still a valid rhythmic structure and can be expressed without metrical limitations. This kind of freedom comes only when the poet's words are freely riding the pulse generated naturally by the poet, and rhythmic structure is unrestricted, even if, at times, our listener absorbs the rhythmic freedom as arrhythmic modulation. So, without complication, I would like to share with you the simplicity of Japanese form poetry in its English equivalent, how it works with or without punctuation and titles, and how you can achieve mastery of Japanese form poetry just by learning form and including some basic form elements in your own poetry. Some Westerners use punctuations, such as commas, or a 2m dash (–) to mark pivotal sections in haiku and other Japanese form poetry, and some, like I, use a vertical caesura mark (| |) in place of commas to mark where one phrase ends and another begins. Some prefer to create without using conventional signs. Nevertheless, to aid you with some basic Japanese terms and history, I have referred to Encyclopedia Britannica, which presents the most easy-to-comprehend authority on Japanese form poetry. With Encyclopedia Britannica's help, this introduction will show various types of Japanese form poetry, how they are interconnected, and how they can be used to create and structure your own poems.

E. Owen

This book is composed of poetic forms that include choka (pronounced chŌ-ka), katauta (pronounced kata-Ūta), haiku and haiku-syllabic form (pronounced hī-ko͞o by Westerners, and "hahy-koo" in Japanese tradition). The latter pronunciation of haiku has 3 "ōn," or stated simply, 3 vowel sounds in the letters a, i, and u, whereas an English pronunciation will have only 2 vowel sounds in the letters i and u, with vowels a and i spoken together as one sound (as in the word hi). Nevertheless, to avoid confusion, I will keep the focus on English language phonetics. The remaining forms covered in this book, although not in this order, are tanka (pronounced TAN-ka), and the American Haiku (the SHST pronounced SHEHst).

Now, let's begin by introducing the term "Waka," which was the name to describe Japanese poetry written for members of a royal household in monarchy, recited at royal court, or for its nobility in the 6th to 14th century. Waka includes such forms as Choka and Sedoka, and reportedly is also used as a synonym for the most basic form of Japanese poetry, the "tanka." Tanka means "Short poem" in Japanese, but let's begin with the choka form and work back to the tanka, to give you a brief history about the choka form, its components, and how those components become interconnected with other forms and essential elements of Japanese form poetry.

Choka

is a Japanese style of long-form storytelling with poetry. The name "Choka" (cho + ka) in Japanese means "long poem." The choka structure can have as many lines as the poet desires,

Mastering Japanese Form Poetry and the American Haiku

traditionally up to 150. Its central theme in this book is love but can be whatever the poet chooses. Nevertheless, it must consist of alternating syllabic lines of 5-7-5, and end with an extra 7-syllable line, which may be followed preferably by one or more additional 7-syllable lines called envoys, or "hanka" in Japanese. Reportedly, modern scholars have suggested that choka originated as recitations of deeds and promises of remembrance to purge the recently departed members of "imperial families" of evil spirits. The new, longer structure seems to have come into court poetry sometime between the 6th and 14th century and allowed traditional poets to explore new themes and expressions formally limited to the rigid, 5-line, 31-syllable tanka form.

Envoy

or hanka lines were used to address the person for whom the choka was written, or to comment on or summarize the body of the poem. With the choka line structure, envoys may vary in number and consist of 7 syllables per line.

The first three lines

of a westernized choka may contain the base clause of the poem and take the form of a katauta-syllabic triplet (KST) about love or a haiku-syllabic triplet (HST) about nature. For clarification, and to distinguish a triplet that does not rhyme from a triplet that does rhyme (for example, a tercet), this book will refer to haiku, katauta, and the first three lines of longer poems, as a triplet and define them according to their 3-line structure, theme and purpose, rather than by rhyming pattern or linear metrical sequence. In this book you will find double and triple HSTs in a single poem or in some way creating hybrid structure within traditional form (see pages 37, 46, and 71). Any triplet type may "begin the journey" to the body of a longer poem in a separate stanza or by remaining connected as part of one continuous verse.

Katauta

is a short, Japanese form of love poem, whose written name curiously comes from the Japanese katakana syllabary, which, before you panic and bail on this segment, is simply a list of written characters used as a type of alphabet to express various elements of borrowed foreign language, slang words, and onomatopoeia, in Japanese terms. Reportedly, the term "Katauta" first appeared in "Man'yō-shū," a 7th century imperial collection of Japanese court poetry and seems to have come from the katakana syllabary in translation from Chinese characters to represent Japanese words phonetically and semantically. "Katauta" in Japanese means "half-poem." The katauta can assume two different syllabic structures (17 and 19 syllables (5-7-5 or 5-7-7)) according to Encyclopedia Britannica, and, based on consensus, katauta were usually addressed to a lover. The 5-7-5 KST reportedly may also have been the first three lines of the tanka, like the hokku (discussed later) was for the renga, but there was no mention that the first three lines of the katauta included a reference to seasons as they do for the renga, which you will also read more about in following segments. Traditionally, love letters were written between love interests using three lines of 19 syllables (5-7-7) for each letter. A single katauta of 19 syllables, however, was considered a half poem or incomplete.

Mastering Japanese Form Poetry and the American Haiku

Therefore, katauta poetry required communication between lovers. Exchanges of the katauta reportedly became longer question-and-answer poems, wherein often poets posed a question and provided an answer to it in the same poem (for example, "How do I love thee? Let me count the ways" by American poet, Emily Dickenson). On the other hand, when two katauta were written between lovers, the 6-line, 38 syllable structure they created was called a sedoka (pronounced seh-dŌ-ka).

Sedoka

(sedo + ka) or "head-repeated poem" consisted of two tercets with a 5-7-7 syllabic line structure. It addressed a lover and rhymed the last word of each line of the 3-line structure. A tercet therefore is a poem of three lines whose last words rhyme. This format distinguishes the tercet from the HST and KST whose linear and syllabic structures are three unrhymed lines, only 17 syllables, and differ restrictively and thematically. So, for the Westerner I am, I have used the 19-syllable, unrhymed katauta (KST) in several 3-line structural poems titled "Love Letter," since they were katauta-syllabic (KS) half poems when I wrote them for lovers. I also used this 19-syllable (KST) format as the "first three lines" to open several choka poems. You can find a Katauta tercet titled "Longing for You" on page 20 of this book.

Tanka

(tan + ka) in Japanese means short poem and "in literary form," historically has been foundational to Japanese form poetry. It is a 5-line, 31-syllable poem whose first three lines consist of a katauta triplet made up of a 5-7-5 syllabic line structure (KST) if the theme is love, or a haiku triplet made up of a 5-7-5 syllabic line structure (HST) if the theme is nature. Both types are followed by the last two lines of 7 syllables each. Notice this form is the alternate of the 5-7-7 syllable katauta triplet (KST) mentioned earlier, and that the name of this triplet changes from haiku-syllabic triplet (HST) to katauta-syllabic triplet (KST) to accord with the katauta's general theme about love; however, there are many themes such as melancholy, joy, humor, and other moods that can be used to create a tanka. Change in theme is the only reasonable explanation for using the 17-syllable line structure for a katauta. Historically, a 5-7-5 triplet is rumored to have been part of the tanka, which later for the first time was referred to as "Renga" in an imperial collection of poems (c. 1125). Renga in Japanese means "linked poetry." The tanka is also a form of linked poetry like the sedoka, because it requires two poets contribute linking verses to complete one poem. With the tanka, unlike with the sedoka, the last two lines of 7 syllables, instead of the last three lines, were written by the second poet in response to the first three lines written by the first poet, who, if so chose, would provide dubious and inconsistent details that challenged the second poet to respond intelligently or creatively. You will find a sample of this katauta style of tanka in "Peace Bond Rose" that shows how the last two lines complete the first three lines of the tanka on page 41. The westernized tanka format, however, may serve as a single 31 syllable love poem written in tanka-syllabic format by one lover to another, to which the other might link with two, three, or five lines. Otherwise, the last

Mastering Japanese Form Poetry and the American Haiku

two lines may refer traditionally to the first three lines before them, or simply continue the theme as a single verse by the second poet using the 5-7-5-7-7 syllabic format to create a renga or two separate tanka. You will find westernized tanka throughout this book. The renga reportedly also supplied the opening triplet in earlier exchanges of longer, question-and-answer "linked verse" written between two or more poets, although not necessarily love interests. In this case, the opening triplet was a haikai or hokku. Thus, at some point in the poem, a kireji (pronounced Ki-re-Ji), which is a fancy word for shift or brake in the poem, was embedded in the first three lines and distinguished the HT from its counterpart, the KT, whose traditional rules do not require mention of a season, and which you will learn more about in the haiku section below. In addition, time of day, and reference to the surrounding landscape is also a thematic tradition when creating a Japanese haiku. When an additional 7-syllable line is attached at the end of a tanka-syllabic quintain ((TSQ) (the five-line tanka stanza)), the tanka is referred to as "Buddha's footprint," according to Encyclopedia Britannica. Its Japanese term is more difficult to pronounce, so I have kept my promise to use an English equivalent. Reportedly, "Buddha's Footprint" is a reference to a set of 21 poems carved on stone kept at Yakushiji Temple in Nara, Japan. You will find the Buddha's Footprint structure in "Ginkgo Love" on page 55. The poem will also show how a haiku triplet (HT) is used to begin a poem, and how the poem becomes hybridized when its theme segues from being about nature to being about love and nature when the last three lines are added.

E. Owen

Haiku

reportedly got its title during the early 1600s to mid-1800s, and the first half of its name was derived from the root portion of the term "haikai." Haikai was the name given to a form of renga poetry if the renga was humorous. The second half of its name derived from the stem portion of the term "hokku." Hokku was the name given to the first three lines, "which set the tone of the renga," and like its current successor, the haiku, was required to include a season, time of day, and the most important feature of the landscape the poet chose to conceptualize. The haikai and hokku apparently shared the prominence of the first three lines of a renga and may have given haiku its name for that reason in the latter part of the 19th century. Currently "haiku" is the term to describe all poems adhering to a 3-line, 17-syllable structure. Traditional haiku poetry is usually a "short poem" (or "short song") about nature. It is composed of 17 syllables with a 5-7-5 syllabic line structure (SLS). The name haiku seems to have been borrowed from Chinese language, which means its origin, "hai ku," as seen written here in two separate terms, is also likely to have been translated by the katakana syllabary. In translation from Chinese, if "hai ku" means "still crying," it is also possible that the two terms were brought together using the katakana syllabary to resolve Chinese semantics, while also deriving at the same time from those earlier terms, haikai and hokku, to name the Japanese haiku that is consistent with today's English translation: "amusement verse," which leads the origin of the name haiku back to the haikai. Reportedly, the hokku was used in the renga the same

Mastering Japanese Form Poetry and the American Haiku

way it was used in tanka and choka forms, with the only difference being the form of poem it opened with its 3-line, 17-syllable structure in choka sequence poetry, instead of in linked poetry such as the tanka. Nevertheless, in Japanese tradition, haiku will include a reference to at least one of the four seasons (winter, spring, summer, fall), time of day (morning, noon, night, or other variants (sunrise, nightfall, twilight)), and a surrounding landscape (a river, trees, a forest, a meadow) to conceptualize the poem's meaning. Traditional Japanese poets placed much emphasis on the "kireji" ("the shift" or "break" in English). A kireji creates a sudden perceptual shift in direction of the poem, but not necessarily a shift in theme, and it is said that its purpose is to conceptualize the meaning of the poem with imagery and epiphany. A kireji can consist of a single word or a string of words to construct the 7-syllable, second line of a haiku. In the westernized haiku, more accurately termed haiku-syllabic triplet (HST), aka, "haiku," a kireji is also called the "cutting word," "break," or "cut-away line." The line or word serves as a pivot to the last line of the HST. The pivot word itself or pivotal words in traditional haiku (TH) is called a "kigo" and can occur at any time in the poem or at the same time the kireji occurs. A kigo can also be the word or words that make up a kireji (or shift). The kigo's purpose in a TH and HST is to refer to a season of the year. For example, a kigo can use the actual name of a season or refer to it descriptively, for example, as "crisp leaves tumble to the ground" to refer to autumn. In this line, "crisp leaves" and "leaves tumble" would be considered kigo(s), because crisp and tumbling leaves are found mostly in autumn. Nevertheless, in westernized haiku, tanka, choka, and katauta form's limiting conditions such as kireji and kigo are often lifted for creative freedom, and an HST may replace a katauta-syllabic triplet (KST) and vice versa for a poet constructing a longer hybrid of more than one theme (e.g., as with "Ginkgo Love"). Also, hybridization does not have to focus necessarily on themes about love and nature; it can focus as well on creativity and embellishment. A poet who begins a poem with an HST can hybridize by including more than one language in the poem. For example, a poet can embellish a poem by adding a line of French or Spanish to make the fourth line of a tanka read or sound more interesting and romantic melodically. Thematic expressions can still be about moods and emotions, like love, sadness, joy, and even humor.

The American Haiku

In addition to syllabic line structure for the traditional Japanese haiku, I have found that Westerners creating contemporary poetry, particularly in the United States, enjoy an uninhibited style of haiku-syllabic triplet (HST) called Senryu (pronounced Sen-rē-ū) and abbreviated SHST (and if desired, pronounced SHEHst) when the S for senryu is added to HST). The westernized senryu-haiku-syllabic triplet (SHST) retains a trace of Japanese tradition in its name and its 3-line, 17-syllable structure, and for incorporating human nature, irony, satire, and cynicism, in its thematic expressions. Whereas traditional Japanese senryu haiku would not incorporate a kigo, Westerners who create SHST poetry take pride in manipulating the kireji to punctuate the pivotal line and conceptualize the poem's punchline and clever meaning.

Mastering Japanese Form Poetry and the American Haiku

At the same time, little attention, if any, is given to whether the SHST includes a traditional form of kigo, even if the poet decides to include seasons in the senryu. The human condition, with all its foibles and braggadocio, seems to be the central theme for the westernized haiku in the United States, and many of its poets are remarkably creative, witty, and clever, with their use of kireji to deliver an "instantaneous fragment of emotion and perception" that is often key when writing American haiku.

Lastly, I have written 130 poems for your reading pleasure, but while you deconstruct them and use them as your guide for better understanding and becoming a master at creating Japanese form poetry, take notice of syllabic line structures and thematic expressions, and try to avoid becoming overly concerned about remembering Japanese labels for different forms of Japanese poetry. Work with one form at a time, and you will find that Japanese language descriptions, form poetry, and structural elements that contribute to form poetry introduced in this book and others, will soon become clear and retainable with practice. You will find that I have used haiku-syllabic line structure with traditional and hybridized themes, and both 5-7-5 and 5-7-7 katauta-syllabic line structures throughout this book for learning consistency and poetic efficacy. Feel free to experiment with original hybrid forms using your own thematic expressions, and, perhaps, add to this 21st-century, contemporary lexicon of English literature made possible because a trend-setting Japanese poet named Matsuo Basho believed that poetry can be executed with freedom, brevity, and fluidity, and still retain conceptual beauty. In his belief, Matsuo Basho broke from centuries-old traditions of rigid conformity to long-form and rhythmic structures by embracing future contemporary poets of our time with his legacy, foresight, and creative vision for the future of poetry. Matsuo Basho is credited with being the founder of the most contemporary form of Japanese haiku enjoyed in the twentieth century. You can learn more about Matsuo Basho from Encyclopedia Britannica.

Happy writing, and good luck!

Mastering Japanese Form Poetry and the American Haiku

Poetry for Lovers Who Write

Complicated

My eyes follow you

savoring every moment

Though I am vain I am lost

astray in silence

in some mysterious way

vain to love you from afar

Though I am careful

minding my p's and my q's

I am without discernment

vain without a plan

Love is more complicated

Please believe my loving heart

share the tenderness of yours

cure my heart of vanity

E. Owen

Love Letter

With this be assured,

I shall be your guardian—

My honor pledged to love you.

Paradox

With this paradox

comes absurdity and love

and balance of complete trust

Yet love is my faith

I have not faith without love

Though I have not religion

love without true faith

absurdity is my fear

that I have been mistaken

I cannot unlove you now

cannot face my greatest fear

Faith and foolishness have won

Mastering Japanese Form Poetry and the American Haiku

Love Letter

Expectation is

love's way of being patient

Reward our will to love

Yearning

To my heart's content

elixir is the warm night

yet all I have is yearning

to belie my heart

is severed || without regret

I am confused what to do

without sedative

to rest my loving heartache

satisfy my yearning thus

Quench this appetence for love

See my eyes give way to urge

Does your heart not thirst for thirst?

E. Owen

It Is Only Fair

By chance I should ask

Is your heart in the right place

I should tell you first

It is only fair this time

I should be the one to tell

my heart is cheating

Though I feel an awful shame

still I am not sure

if that shame is in my heart

or wholly passing

Should I be ashamed to love

Can my heart cheat and not stray

taste sweetness without her fruits

tell me lies and still be round

Longing for You

Absent from my bed

my own breathing thus I wed

longing for your love instead

Mastering Japanese Form Poetry and the American Haiku

With You

I can feel romance

affect for the little things

wanting nothing for myself

Without Love

How do I proceed

withered without your sweet smile

orchid without sun

How shall I endure

on rainy days without you

Love is all I know

surely as with night and day

Lover I am lost

on the outside peering in

a heart without you to love

Will you give my heart comfort

fellow feeling for my plight

Will you lie with me till dawn

E. Owen

Kiss Me

Had my share || Good night

of brag and fragrant Holly

I want Summer Snow.

Seemly Hearts

Induced by her kiss

my senses were aroused and

crave her endlessly

Woman has seduced my heart

I also to blame

easy like a harlot's core

bedded for the joy she brings

I am nonchalant

sinning after lust for her

Should I not play unconcerned

though seemly hearts cannot be

lie thus to my modest heart

that my sinner is my soul

Mastering Japanese Form Poetry and the American Haiku

The KSTs below reconceptualize the balcony scene from Shakespeare's "Romeo and Juliet," replicating Shakespearean vernacular in a coquettish parody, wherein the young lovers replace tragedy with contentment. I hope you will enjoy Romeo & Juliet in KST.

Juliet Teases

Wherefore, Romeo,

your journey hence? Have I not

forsworn of thy love?

Romeo Persistent

If Juliet's heart

thus swore, my journey is false,

yet my heart still pure.

Romeo Continues

Can it yet be said

lips journey to their kisses,

travels unsurpassed?

E. Owen

Juliet

Unsurpassed indeed,

yet journey not to kisses.

I beseech you. Come!

Romeo Hesitates

What pray, Juliet,

say you to stranded hearts that

love without consent?

Juliet Replies

Romeo is fair,

yet thy heart's cordage is not

with mine so stranded.

Romeo's Heart

My true love mocks me,

yet she spake of it. Stranded

is not forsaken.

Mastering Japanese Form Poetry and the American Haiku

Juliet's Heart

Abandon me not,

for I am content stranded

If indeed plaited.

Romeo's Oath

Upon stranded oath

that my love and oath are true,

I shall not leave thee.

Juliet's Answer

And leave the Black Rod's

sword off thy head ere you kneel

before my father?

Romeo's Fate

Black Rod's sword or not,

my fate has cursed my presence

before his Lordship.

E. Owen

Juliet

Pray thee away now.

Hide thee in the black night, lest

you cause me sorrow.

Romeo's Good Night

My head will take leave,

not my heart from Black Rod's sword.

Till morrow, sweet love.

Juliet Pauses

Would not thy heart run

upon Black Rod's sword give it pause—

and thy love for me?

Romeo Vows

Black Rod nor repose

shall I leave pause my love. My

love is eternal.

Mastering Japanese Form Poetry and the American Haiku

Juliet Next Morning

Good morrow, my love,

for thy precious smile I did

but watch the night long.

Romeo

But peace too soon, for

I must tend my flank, lest my

wake consume thy watch.

Juliet

My father loves thee,

not thy father's name, but watch,

soon he will amend.

Romeo Ascends

Watch beyond while I

ascend for morrow's kiss. Wait!

Heard I your father?

E. Owen

Juliet

Watch! My nurse. My kiss?

He has to market 'til noon.

Lie with me 'til then?

Romeo Past Noon

Watch! The sun has turned,

and I my fill yet hunger.

And she—Juliet?

Juliet

I tend her watch to

cleave, and she hungers more to

purge her lust with love.

Juliet (Next Day)

Romeo, doth My

Lord hence give event thy heart's

swell for thy lover?

Mastering Japanese Form Poetry and the American Haiku

Romeo

Let hearts do as hearts

will, lest we follow devout

their bidding events.

Juliet

Are hearts not foolish

folly without true love and

true love's heart's event?

Romeo's Troth

Then, my true love, I

troth my heart's event to thee

and love no other.

Juliet

A woman's heart knows

no greater event than love—

and now Romeo.

E. Owen

Romeo Next Day

Fair, Juliet! Speak!

Last kiss is but vintage fruit.

Pray thy love renew.

Juliet's Nurse

For truth, My Lord, she

has to a nunnery. Her

vintage father's wish.

Romeo's Sorrow

Good nurse, say you lie!

For vintage pain restores to

my once happy heart.

Juliet's Nurse

"With deepest sorrow,"

the vintage of my words are

from your Juliet.

Mastering Japanese Form Poetry and the American Haiku

Romeo's Farewell to Juliet

Till thy love's vintage

bends thy river's journey hence,

farewell my true love.

Juliet's Nurse

Then take thy sorrow

and mourn thy love, else take her

vintage her return.

Romeo

Nurse, by what season

canst thou prove her return hence?

She has spoken thus?

Juliet's Nurse

Season without time

is without occasion, as

love without nurture.

E. Owen

Romeo Confused

Wherefore doth thou speak

with unseasoned tongue? Have you

word from Juliet?

Juliet's Nurse

She is betrothed, sir.

Seasoned, not married to Duke

of York. She loves <u>you</u>.

Juliet Returns

Hence unseasoned to

fare thee well with great sorrow.

My heart prays forgive.

Romeo's Pride

I know not season

nor suitable occasion—

I know not forgive.

Mastering Japanese Form Poetry and the American Haiku

Juliet's Sorrow

Then forgive not if

thou know not how, and I will

away with my love.

Romeo's Reply

Know not and will not,

and come what season shall, I

shall with thee always.

Juliet's Joy

Then blossom season

her flower with love. I am

ever after yours.

The end

Word Prompts: Journey, stranded, black, pause, watch, event, vintage, and season, for Romeo * Juliet in KST were provided by @Baffled for #haikuchallenge at www.twitter.com

E. Owen

Missed Heaven

I want you so much

Lend to your heart my love or

my heaven is missed

my reasons without basis

my love without love

ever stranded in my dreams

wishing they were true

clinging to your slender hands

coupled on my face

Tender kisses on my lips

my lover awakens me

Have I left one love to dream?

Don't Go!

Tasted saline tears,

thousand wishes in a stream

My first time in love.

Sacred Heart

Seldom spoke of us

of intimacy we shared

lest I lose your love

to betray your sacred heart—

excited amongst my peers

stirring their senses

that love vicariously

Our necks become their kisses

noses meeting with

bouquets for my true love || Their

lips inspired part

jealous lovers one and all

long before I let you down

Can you ever forgive me?

E. Owen

Connecting

Holding steadily,

devastated without you,

until I see you again.

Allow Me

Let me show you love

take you down to river's flow

place your mind at ease

Warm your precious tender heart

find your way with me

all the ways that I can love

Cast off all your fears

I will keep you warm and safe

soothe your tender loins

taste the sweetness of your thighs

persist upon your frenzy

Any chance you will consent

to let your heart speak with love

Mastering Japanese Form Poetry and the American Haiku

Our Talks

I am still tingling

You were terrific last night—

Been a long time since we talked.

Sun-lit Moon

Moon-lit summer night

golden pathway to the shore

shimmers on the sea

Sun-lit moon half full

lovers stroll along the shore

ripples at their feet

crystals on their naked soles

Are they contemplating love?

Call

Give me just one call

Tell me that the time is right

I promise not to tarry

E. Owen

I Love You

Sometimes you do not

occupied by inner thoughts

know how much I do

Say nothing of specific

little things we share

curling corners when we smile

listening with hearts

making precious moments last

holding onto thoughts

I just wanted you to know

sometimes I need you to know

Not Like That

Just the other day

seems to set quite well with me

looking forward to the next

Mastering Japanese Form Poetry and the American Haiku

Candid Poses

I love watching you

fishing for that thing misplaced

Where could it have gone

Swishing round inside your purse

standing on one leg

worries balanced on one knee

candid poses unconfined

When you notice I am there

your face lights up with a smile

that sooner pouts than lingers

till I am emoting too

How can I bring you comfort

find your glasses on your head

without causing you chagrin

E. Owen

Chagrin

I am so ashamed

whirling weather tulips bend

yearning evermore

But for yearning lover's heart

I am guilty on my own.

Peccant Lines

Should I feel awful

loving you just for myself

I do not recall

when love crossed the peccant line

or sinned without purge

when punition changed a heart

when lovers were so dispensed

to abandon their true love

I am not discrete in this

I can love no other way

Mastering Japanese Form Poetry and the American Haiku

Peace Bond Rose

Petalled spring flower

tender loving consort || thus

will I surrender

secrets of a chosen heart

that loves you more completely

Yellow Petal

Thanks-giving season

cornucopia for love

mirth of sugar fruits

Something new late November

masking whom we are

loving deeper than before

kisses just as sweet

yellow petal in the sun

stronger than the hurried wind

We still have the course of time.

E. Owen

M

Yes || I do recall

when my heart first tasted love

nibbling heedlessly

like sampling sweet chocolates

never satisfied

needing all the attention

jealously at times

more afraid of losing love

You were life to me

love and orb and maiden hair

enduring in only love

Forgive me for letting go.

Love Floods

Her place and mine || a

passage worth the journey and

flooding gates with love.

Mastering Japanese Form Poetry and the American Haiku

A Love for Spring

Monocots in bloom

apical stems anew || Be

still my heart for spring

I have tasted my true love

summoned whispers from her heart

Softly

Mimosa melting

tulips when they kiss do tell

but sweetly unknown

to but lady love perhaps

shedding in due course her veil

Accidental Love

In between the words

Where I find your meaning lost

Blame me and bathetic love.

E. Owen

Yes

In winter and spring

love flowers in sun and rain

You should know by now

Nocturnal Flower

I desire just

one wish that fleeting reveals

your petals unfold—

warm heart receptive to love

I can think of nothing else.

Mm Yes

Mm chrysanthemum

stirring curiosity

Am I still in love

all I am within your name?

Can I make things right for us?

Mastering Japanese Form Poetry and the American Haiku

Trust

What rose by other

mocks true love and is still true

What a foul is trust

that trusts my heart not to love

someone else I cannot have

Resignation

I can love you more

conjure with deep compassion

redefine my thoughts

of what a true love should be

resign to love only you

Love Letter

I never used you

found whatsoever folly

where knowingly I found love

E. Owen

Love Chooses

If we choose || why do

we fall || sacrifice ourselves

dare to repeat once

our hearts have been broken?

Dare we choose to fall again?

Secrets

Mark my velvet tongue

measure my affection thus

touch your hand to mine

Slink and tow and stay

sweet concessions as you will

breathe me into love

Secrets tell their names

discretely like quick kisses

whispered from their lips

Mastering Japanese Form Poetry and the American Haiku

Oh Gahd Daamn!

Lilacs bloom like sweet

love labors for breath and calls

the whirling wild wind

Catch your breath and stay with me

turn into the wind

swearing toward the morning sun

racing toward the dawn

Love beyond break of the day

well into the light

firmly tender in my arms

fingers in my hair

kiss me over your shoulder

I am yours with all my strength.

Love Letter

I have incurred this

thus the pillory enfolds

my heart content with its sin

E. Owen

Uncertainty

My heart I fear weeps

oftentimes confusing me

I choose to love yet

linger with uncertainty

abandoned by my own heart

Love in Winter

Cold and briskly harsh

winter stirring hawkishly

chilling to the bone

makes for perfect time to love

May I spend some time with you

Comfort Me

Cupped your tender hands

placed upon my bearded cheek

thus take their fill my sorrow

I forever pledge my love

with your consent is worthy

Mastering Japanese Form Poetry and the American Haiku

Willing

With new affection

I am pusillanimous

yet therefore willing

to overcome my fears but

my timid heart makes me wait

Imperfect

"Were man but constant

he were perfect" lover's heart

before and after

untorn between desire

first for one than another

Loveless

Stranger than fiction

a heart without conviction

ailment without prescription

E. Owen

Lie with Me

Will you honor me

lie with me just for tonight

I want you to stay

You will never have to leave

never hear the words good-bye

Come Over

Can you come over

stop by my place for awhile

so I can hold you

make a special meal for you

Dessert will be your preferred

Imbue Me

If you persuade me

imbue me with all your wiles

what shall be my task

Settle with your inner thoughts

Use me to your heart's content

Mastering Japanese Form Poetry and the American Haiku

If Love Declared

What if love declared

contemplating as I do

words | would it relate

how thoughts of you bring me joy

how your love completes my life

Whisper

Hold your cheek to mine

pass the time of day with me

whisper something sweet

find yourself in love's embrace

I have waited all my life

Tuesdays

Tuesdays in the fall

leaves in battle with the wind

shudder from the breeze

stimulating merry moods

love enkindling holocaust

E. Owen

Cheated Heart

Perchance I hold forth

confessing love for you || thus

cheating on myself

blabbing on my cheating heart

will you still consent to love

No Pride

If you take my heart

amble with me hand in hand

I will not saunter

have not dignity nor pride

need nothing except your love

Mastering Japanese Form Poetry and the American Haiku

Making Plans

Autumn's briskly breath

swishing round her shed green leaves

wheeling at your feet

scolded plaited locks undone

not much time for talk

Are we other than the leaves?

Are we contemplating love?

Distant Lover

Let us fall in love

when we meet between the lines

touching lips with words

celebrating life and love

soothing distant lover's hearts

E. Owen

Envy

Silky narratives

light feet on 24-Mo

you make me jealous

wishing I had written lines

with such eloquence

Envious pen || jealous heart

like wishful thinkers

watching lovers make their peace

awing with their tears

reminiscing sweeter times

coveting || I love you more

needing to succeed somehow

Will you comfort me tonight

Guilty Pleasure

My one heart is torn

yet I know too well my place

For that I suffer

conflicted guilty pleasure

Mastering Japanese Form Poetry and the American Haiku

that my eager eyes behold
uncertain beyond my reach
awaiting your sweet consent
Will there be a time for us?
Will I know your loving heart?

Ginkgo Love
Leaf of Maidenhair
wafted from the highest tree ||
Twilight in the Spring
lovers browse till after sun
has set the painted heaven
before darkness and rebirth

The Way We Do
Cold wind on my face
I glance into the sunlight
Where could you have gone
Chance to say "hello"
vanished hopelessly at once

E. Owen

sooner than my fear

Somehow have I offended

somehow lost my way

Perhaps I should have waited

Thought you would return

have a talk the way we do ||

a little laughter

reminisce of better times

Every thought is you

Tell me what is mint for now

I only want to listen

Am I worthy of your time?

Fun

Like catching moments

of sun and naughty ideas ||

this one for lovers

Their trysts for fun and secrets

to their hearts be their content

To their content be their love

Mastering Japanese Form Poetry and the American Haiku

Unloved

Thus is he unloved

Sleepless slumber less a friend

colder than half-moon

till summer comes past waning

August floral skirt

buttons down the one-gore welt

teases me with love

stretches long the moon-lit shore

My thoughts are with her always.

Lotus Lover

I need tenderness

supple fingers on my face

warm breath when we kiss

love that from a muddied toil

rises with new sun

like lotus lilies reborn

like first footsteps on new Earth

A lover that offers love ||

E. Owen

Moments after seeming lost ||

a purpose that will not fade

I want to be your lover.

I want to be your lover.

Her

Screed loving her tongue

sheer diaphanous sleeper

goose pimples aside

I press my ear to her words

lean in to whispers

certain they will call my name

like casting love in

silhouette and silk-chiffon

I caress her curves

fingers trembling to touch her

nibbling through the silk

farther past the gathered hem

I Kiss below her pelvis

gather seashells on the way

to warm and loving furrows

tucking gently || settling in ||

thankful for love and patience

Saturated With Love

Learning my lover

she teaches me to love her

how to touch her skin

combine in love with patience ||

open all the more

like seraphim's emotions

rapacious lover

saturating me with love

coursing like rivers through me

Every emotion winding

not a single moment still

I cannot catch and hold them

They make me stretch and curl them

compel me when to breathe

compel me to hold my breath

E. Owen

stiffen me and thicken me

till the final sigh is cast

Yin and Yang

Tell me about love

time of water in the air

when I need you most

Slink your body close to mine

cheek against my cheek

receptive to my kisses

browsing to your breasts

Slender fingers down my back

breast to navel kiss

pelvic writhing when we stir

like moving meditation

grasping sparrow's tail

Lady shuttling side to side

waxing and waning

till the cosmos is at peace

If ever you have known love

Mastering Japanese Form Poetry and the American Haiku

now is the time to tell me

Waxing Poetic

Serifs trailing lines

gliding like ocean rhythm

riding waves to shore

Similes glance and then strut

Across 24's

dance on headers and footers

streak and then linger

making love then repeating

Baby I love you

on hot summer days and nights

Beaded fingertips

wet with love's perspiration

drip || drip || drip || dripping

Bellies clapping || silver beads

still wet collapsing

Rising || clinging || muscles tense

E. Owen

Erogenous verses brief

Breathless expressions terse like:

C'mon baby || You like that ||

Oh that's good || Oh damn that's good

Rearing back and breathing strained

Roaring toward the last exhale

speechless restless breathing done

I have to go to work now

I'll see you when you get home

Candid Stare

Thoughts of only you

candid images in love

I began to stare

You gave me purpose || I am

beside myself over you

Mastering Japanese Form Poetry and the American Haiku

No Place to Go

Outside in the cold

skeleton-like limbs branching

reaching overhead

fruitless if not for lovers

leaning on her bark

tasting sweet maple syrup

with light amber lips

floating softly on warm breath

Palms reaching || cupping haunches

Shoulders high || heads careening

tilting lovers into love

Thawing frigid gales recede

lovers with no place to go

E. Owen

Lovers Till Dawn

Lamplight on still pond

yielding to lilies and stone

rooted in mire

Lesser similes describe

ever-lasting love

Never-ending lovers bend

capture sunlight in the moon

Sempiternal like the stars

we were lovers till new dawn

Love Letter

My thoughts deny me

conjuring like obsession—

woman inveigling logic

Mastering Japanese Form Poetry and the American Haiku

Metaphor for Love

Write my name in love

touch my heart with tenderness

I will surrender

Meet me on a sunlit shore

gazing at the sea

while my tender heart awaits

metaphor for love

Wrap me in your tender gaze

soft and kindly words

hearten my devotion with

similes for love

Leap with faith like nightingales

sparrows and the lark

Trust that I will love you with

all my heart and strength

that I might forever sore

like nightingales and sparrows

E. Owen

For Lovers Only

One petal remains

summerly emblem for love

so say lovers' hearts

Jumbled sprigged hieroglyphs

spelling "I love you"

yet my heart is not misled

Tepals sometimes lie

speak of love with cheating hearts

Sepals keep them safe

Somehow lovers know flowers

only lovers' hearts can find

I Do

When you think of me

do love's emotions flood you

cascade from within

like rivers overflowing

Do you thirst despite the flood?

Mastering Japanese Form Poetry and the American Haiku

Plump for Love

Dogwood winter snow

rosy flower's petals fall

Lovers promenade

Those who wander when they stroll

their tender paces

mingling with the vernal night

tending to their thoughts

seldom plump for one-night stands

set their hearts on lasting love

Father Time

Fear not her autumn

her cycle everlasting

She is womanhood

a winter in cessation

proliferative in Spring

summer full of life and joy

E. Owen

Still My Heart

You know I love you

No longer should we pretend

we do not have time

cannot make a time for love

knowing what we want

Love has not been lost on us

My eyes search for you

wherever I find myself

alone without love

There is pain in this torn heart

without you to love

Paramour and still my heart

though it suffers still loves you

Mastering Japanese Form Poetry and the American Haiku

Unloved Heart

That look in her eyes

quite certain of her station

unrelenting gaze

as certain as with lovers

knowing whom to trust

whom trusting fails betrayal

she leads with her heart

Thus I am left to wonder

knowing as I do

steering words away from love

holding tight my tongue

have I left a heart unloved

Have I ever been unkind

E. Owen

Never Have Never Will

Strange feeling today

cannot call it this or that ||

never have I loved

I would know had I succumb

drifted from her care

ravaged by vacuity

cornered like a sod

trembling while the spirits fade

though the sun is high

certain love is sober yet

I have known first-hand

Never have abandoned love

Never will abandon love ||

willing to be loved again

Mastering Japanese Form Poetry and the American Haiku

Your Love and I

With my heart I know

love is much more than I feel

more than I can hold

yet so calm and so serene

moving standing still

moving me to love you more

staying with me || flooding life

with overwhelming

motion and stillness and what

if not our love ||

Might we find ourselves alone

sailing on sun waves

surfing lifeless seas

in motion just for rhythm

will you give us thought?

Ever think your love and I?

E. Owen

From Me to You

I thought of daisies

last image of morning moon

fading into day

Perennial season bracts

petals filled with sun

crafted by my kindly hand

No dogwood leaf first in spring ||

daisies for your loving thoughts ||

just a thought from me to you

Esoteric crafty lines

can say so much for lovers

The other language is true

Is it thus for lover lone?

Can one and every partake?

Are love and poetry one?

Mastering Japanese Form Poetry and the American Haiku

Lily Daffodil

My heart is lonely

white as lily daffodil

delicate to touch

My loving heart is with you

I recall your smile

careful way you called my name

I never let go ||

reminisce your tender words

saying whatever

Never meant to let you down

I was drawn to you ||

committed the day we met

committed the more this day

Thank you for finding my heart.

E. Owen

Reborn

After wintry frost

I see your smile in flowers ||

garnish for the sun

White and yellow daffodils

reborn in the Spring

vicarious for lovers

reborn into love

leaning without reflection

I see only you

I can think of no one else.

I suppose I am in love.

Give Me Courage

My conscience laid bare

I steal into loving you

carefree but afraid

uncertain what lies ahead

Give me courage to love you.

Lovers' Twilight

Civil twilight dawn

sunrise with morning kisses

I am late for work

Reasons false as usual

they will one day out

consequential just perhaps

with a smile or two

memories obliging me

Stubborn I am that

destined to repeat the lies

She keeps her own time

Bet he wishes he could stay

She knows well my tender heart

besotted with each twilight

E. Owen

Noble Heart

Impromptu lover

I could not wait to love you

I was insecure

pretending to know the way

What a dope was I

to think love would surrender

to a noble heart

that never once surrendered

never tasted love

until kissed for the first time

You did that for me

asking nothing in return

You were right to let it go

You did the right thing for me

I will always love you first.

Mastering Japanese Form Poetry and the American Haiku

Sources

@Baffled https://www.twitter.com

Choka, Encyclopedia Britannica

Encyclopedia Britannica, Inc. 24 November 1999

https://www.britannica.com/art/choka

Access Date: February 27, 2022

Haikai, Encyclopedia Britannica

Encyclopedia Britannica, Inc. 24 August 2018

https://www.britannica.com/art/haikai

Access date: February 27, 2022

Haiku, Encyclopedia Britannica

Encyclopedia Britannica, Inc. 10 November 2021

https://www.britannica.com/art/haiku

Access Date: February 27, 2022

Japanese Literature. Encyclopedia Britannica

Encyclopedia Britannica, Inc., 25 July 2016

https://www.britannica.com/art/Japanese-Literature

Access Date: January 27, 2022

Katauta, Encyclopedia Britannica

Encyclopedia Britannica, Inc. 01 September 1999

E. Owen

https://www.britannica.com/art/katauta

Access Date: February 28, 202

Poetry. Encyclopedia Britannica

Encyclopedia Britannica, Inc., 18 August 2021.

https://www.britannica.com/art/poetry

Access Date: February 27, 2022

Renga, Encyclopedia Britannica

Encyclopedia Britannica, Inc. 04 December 2016

https://www.britannica.com/art

Access Date: February 27, 2022

Senryu, Encyclopedia Britannica

Encyclopedia Britannica, Inc. 21 January 2015

https://www.britannica.com/art/senryu

Access Date: February 27, 2022

Shakespeare. Two Gentlemen from Verona.

All Great Quotes. https://www.allgreatquotes.com/topis/life-qu...

@AllGreatQuotes www.twitter.com

Access Date: March 28, 2022

Tanka, Encyclopedia Britannica

Mastering Japanese Form Poetry and the American Haiku

Encyclopedia Britannica, Inc. 01 December 2016

https://www.britannica.com/art/tanka-Japanese-poetry

Access Date: February 27, 2022

Waka, Encyclopedia Britannica

Encyclopedia Britannica, Inc. 29 January 1999

https://www.britannica.com/waka-Japanese-poetry

Access Date: February 27, 2022

Appendix

SHEST

5 syllables: Left her standing there
7 syllables: among the barren Maple
5 syllables: I felt like a sap

Haiku about nature

5 syllables:

7 syllables:

5 syllables:

Haiku about love and nature

5 syllables:

7 syllables:

5 syllables:

Mastering Japanese Form Poetry and the American Haiku

NOTES

E. Owen

NOTES

www.ingramcontent.com/pod-product-compliance
Lightning Source LLC
Chambersburg PA
CBHW070855050426
42453CB00012B/2224